A Journey Through My Eyes:
The Hopeless Romantic Edition

BY LEASHA A. SMALL

A Journey Through My Eyes:
The Hopeless Romantic Edition

Written By: Leasha A. Small
Photo Cred: Leasha A. Small & Kieran Khan

This book is presented to
The Hopeless Romantic:

Grab a glass of wine... well, in this case, the bottle and
let's dive in.
Let's toast to a new beginning and lets manifest it
into greatness. I trust we will be guided and blessed
every step of this wonderful journey.
HAPPY READING!!

Acknowledgements

I would like to express my love and gratitude to the following people:
Heather Small my loving mother who literally is the reason I began, not only writing again but compiling all my past and present pieces. Thank you for believing in me.
My Fiancé, Anthony Whilby for being my soundboard to bounce ideas off of. As well as my pillar of strength throughout this process. Thank you for understanding and supporting my creative flow.
My Best friend, the Wife Alyssa Lopez, who has been my shoulder to lean on and my ear from the very beginning. Thank you.
My two cousins Erica and Adriana who have been so supportive of me finally finishing this project thank you both for everything.
Last but not least my family and friends for always believing in me and standing behind me and most importantly God for guiding the way and always being the light through this tunnel.
There are so many others to thank but I am ever so grateful for all the love and support you have all shown.

Introduction

Through the good bad and the ugly, exploring all about love and relationships, with free thoughts, quotes, letters, short tales, poetic, motivational and inspirational pieces that tell the tales of real-life situations through my eyes. These pieces come from things I have gone through, witnessed or heard about. My mission is to give individuals something real they can relate to on this journey through my eyes. A book for the hopeless romantic, broken-hearted, and the ones open to trying this thing we call love again.

Who so loves believes the impossible

Through It All

Love me through the pain.
Hold my hand and tell me
everything is going to be okay.
Comforting words to ease this pain,
from lips of love that keep me sane.
Wrap your arms around me and
hold on tight, as we fall into REM
and slip into the night.
3:08am

Dear Relationship Goals

I don't ever expect perfection and in this day and age how can you, we're only human. As long as two people together are walking towards their goals, holding each other down keeping it 100, that's all that one can ask for. Match my ambition, hell ill match yours. I'm always looking to improve as long as we're working together ill never give up. Let's show and prove, facing the world just us two.

3:50am

Mix It Up

A little bit of me mixed in you.
A combination of love, the perfect
blend of just us two.
Where love becomes the glue, to
bond me and you.
9:55pm

HERE WE GO
AGAIN WITH
YOUR MIXED
SIGNALS AND
MY SECOND
THOUGHTS

UNKNOWN

Scared

Scared to love again she had been through it all. Built up of fear, she didn't know how to let him in. He tried to make her see that he was one of the best but all she could hear was something much less. Not interested in trying, not even for the good guy. He told her a love like this was worth trying but she kept feeling that something was underlying.

2:30am

Slave of Her Past

A victim of her past she had become so broken, bound she had become captive. She never knew she could find a new guy after all this time. He came in, and suddenly everything felt right. How did he know she needed a Mr. Right? Failed attempts at love, she felt like she would never get this thing right. He came along and erased her past, for hopes of the future they would build to last.

3:00am

Busy Lied

I needed you at a time when my heart couldn't rest when my mind played tricks. I needed you more than anything. Didn't you tell me you'd be there, didn't you tell me I was your world and now I can't even buy a chance to cry on the shoulder that once blanketed my tears.

We set out on these seven seas together, hand in hand fighting to make it, and now I'm left in this cold world all alone. I'm lost without you wondering where I went wrong. You say it ain't me, and that we're just busy, but busy lives never told me you wouldn't be here. Busy lives never said you'd take your love away and it never said id be here alone fighting back these tears on my own. Busy lives fooled me, and when I needed you the most busy lives lied to me and told me you were too busy, shame on me.

5:57am

Dead Love On A String

He played the role so well, had me
believing while he was cheating and
suddenly I found myself creeping.
Holding on to a love that once was
strong but still felt myself moving on.
Our love had gone out the window but
yet I felt like the asshole.
When did we both give up the will to try
to make things right?
When did this love up and die?
9:12 am

The Fine Print

Over and over she was trampled with his lies, for all he had was negativity in his eyes. He destructively blew up all her hopes and dreams of walking down the aisle, happy as can be. He knew only she could handle his sporadic modes, so he pushed her away so she couldn't get close. Why she kept going back is a mystery infact, love can blind you make sure to read the fine print of the contract.

2:21pm

Broken Thoughts

When you left you took everything with you, that part of my soul that bleeds you. You took the better half of me. Now I sit and waste away hours, days, and months longing to fast forward through all the hurt that has been done. You promised you wouldn't take your love away, and just as the seasons changed April turned into May. You told me you were here to stay. Why did I believe you when you told me you'd never leave me this way? , My heartaches, and my soul cries out. What am I to do when your not here to help me figure this out. Left alone with a broken heart that seems impossible to mend. How come love leaves us on opposite ends?

11:24pm

About Enough

She put up with so much until enough was enough. He messed up this time and lost her for good. No more meaningless sorries, no more heartless apologies, no more shut up gifts, trips or surprises her love could no longer buy him time. She was done and done for good. What took some time was now finalized. Enough was just enough and this time she said goodbye.

9:41pm

MY HEART
FLATLINED BUT
SOMEHOW I
FEEL MORE
ALIVE
LEASHA A. SMALL

Fight Scene

She knows her attitude is like a ninja in the night, no stopping her when her mouth takes flight. She sees his pain displayed upon his face, but somehow she continues anyway. No stopping the mileage of her attack, for every sentence is like a scene out of mortal combat. He takes her pain and sits back for he knows it's all just an act.

12:00am

You Can't Save Me

I want to scream but that doesn't mean you'll hear me. I want my pain to be understood but that doesn't mean you can save me. I want my tears to be ones of joy but that doesn't mean you can fill this void. I'm stuck and all I can say is what bad luck to meet a man perfect for me but somehow just can't help me.

3:22am

Poker Face

You're poker face was a good one.

I need to applaud you for that run, comedy was your act hun.

Had me thinking I was the one.

Fooled me with your words, played me like a nerd, even had me lost in your world.

Soon enough it will be your turn trust me you will learn.

3:26am

LOVING
YOU WAS A
FOOLISH
GAME THAT
I DECIDED
TO PLAY
LEASHA A. SMALL

He Isn't Them

It's not his fault they did you wrong.
Yet you punish as if it was him.
No man should ever raise his hand to a Queen.
Scared is all you can be. He holds your
emotions delicately in his hands. He knows
what you have gone through, he's sad for you.
He wants you to see it isn't in him to hurt you.
He wasn't raised to cause pain. Instead, he
takes his time to show you, love. He waits
patiently for you to accept his tender warmth
and touch.
He waits patiently for you to see he isn't
them.
10:23 pm

Can You Hear Me

I hope he comes in like Clark Kent to Lois
Lane.
I hope he fights for my heart like sailor moon
in the moonlight.
I hope he crushes obstacles like Stone Cold
Stunner in the ring.
I hope he steals kisses from any angle like
Peter Parker to Gwen Stacey.
And at the end of the day, I hope he connects
with my heart like the perfect Tetris piece, at
the very last minute.

4:24am

Final Wave

If he had paid attention when he had her,
another man wouldn't be able to grab her.
Snatch her up and romance her. Too busy
adding to the lies, he hadn't realized she'd said
her final goodbye.
Oh when will men realize?
11:18 pm

Untitled Tears

That feeling when you're past the point of being sad. So hurt inside, you just want to si
and cry, but you know you can't so you continue moving through the day holding back the tears. That empty life numbing feeling, as you take things day by day, until that one weak moment when the memories take over and the tears run down your face.

8:07 pm

A Jokers Game

He built her up filling her void, little did she know that when he left she would be destroyed. She never took the time to work on herself, emptiness was the hand she was dealt. He played the game and to no surprise, he turned up a winner every time. She longed for a king to sweep her up, but it was her mind that needed to be cleaned up. She lacked self-worth, so every card was to his advantage, she was too blind to see past his advances. Loneliness is not what one desires but single life is what was required. It's time for her to get it together or be lost in this game forever, forever, forever, ever, ever, ever.

(Kanye West Voice)

3:03 am

Just So It's Clear

I long to find a real love.
I mean I'm not on a daily search but I'm open to
the idea of it.
Time and time again I remind myself that I am
deserving of real love, true love, that forever type
of love.
Does it really even exist?
Well, I hope so because in the movies it looks like
real life bliss.
I haven't encountered it quite yet but I'm sure it's
on its way.
12:09am

STARTING OVER IS
NEVER EASY
BUT IT'S NOT
IMPOSSIBLE IF THAT'S
THE CHOICE YOU
WANT
TO MAKE
LEASHA A. SMALL

Aftermath

Give me back the moments you robbed me of.
The memories you helped create and took
away, the ones that haunt me causing me to
have restless sleepless nights. Don't you see
what you have done, causing so much pain?
When will this emptiness I face fade away?
Give me back those moments I long for, the
ones I put in that time for.
Don't I deserve to hold on to them, aren't they
mine?
I spent so much damn time.
1:08am

Set Myself Free

It took sometime to realize walking away from him wasn't about giving up. The moment I decided to set myself free, I birthed a better me. His abuse took a toll on me but as I turned my back and walked away I knew that this was for me. So I could live again, so I could trust again, so I could learn to open up my heart and try to love again.

This is for a new and improved me, so I set myself free.

1:09am

Our Place

I want to take his stress away, be his happy getaway. Let him find his peace in me, tame tha wild beast. Take him to a special place, where h and I can elevate. A place we can't be found, a place on solid ground.

2:19am

Wrong or
Right

It felt so right you and I but deep down we knew this thing just wasn't right. You're not mine and because of that we could never take flight. Love on cloud 9, we couldn't deny but being a passenger on your ride just wasn't right. Right cloud wrong time.

10:43pm

Redirect

One promise after the next followed by an I'm sorry.
How many times can one utter the same words
with no meaning?
Each promise backed with less and less substance,
it grew tired long ago.
The pain continues to run deep and eventually,
each word became less desirable to me.
Until one day the phone calls stopped ringing,
instead sent straight to voicemail.
Blocked!!
No more will broken promises and tired sorries be
heard.
That's the stance I'm willing to take in order to be
heard.
1:05am

LOVE IS NEVER WASTED FOR ITS VALUE DOES NOT REST UPON RECIPROCITY

C.S. LEWIS

Heat of The Moment

He touched me in places that awakened my soul.
He kissed me and made me lose all control.
His eyes took me on an adventure as his hands
started to venture.
Sweat glistening in the night, hearts beating so on
point.
He let me share a piece of his heaven as we stayed
up until 7.
Gazing out into the sky, sun rising time sure does
fly.
Just one night we can't deny.
8:00am

Embodied

Stimulating conversation is what I require, make
my mind spin, forming knowledge from within.
Teach me a little something, educate my mind,
and bring life to the woman in me.
Here he comes speaking life into my soul.
Knowledge igniting the fire with words that I so
require. His mentality is like no other, a fine wine
in which I desire.

1:03am

Wanting Me
Like I Want
You

I want to know that I mean something more to you in
this world, that somewhere beyond our feet you see
more of a future with me. I want you to want me, even
become a little scared at the thought of losing me. I
want to know that talking to me brings you joy and tha
I add extra beats to the rhythm of your heart palpation
That one day without me is a day too long, but worth it
for the anticipation of our next date. I want the
butterflies in my stomach to feel comforted by how
tightly you squeeze me into your chest.
I want my cheekbones to rise as the edges of my lips
curve into a smile when you kiss my forehead. I want
you and only you at the beginning, middle and end of
my days. Somewhere in all of that, I'm just hoping you
want me too.

1:53am

Love Song

His love was like clockwork, it hit strokes with every passing minute. Not a second offbeat, for his love, was always in key. Reaching up-tempos to please me, he'd make me scream like Mariah Carey.
For his love was like a soulful melody, something like some sweet RnB.

1:00am

Lost

I want to get lost in your eyes, letting hours pass us by, unaware of the time.

From day to night I want to be the stars in your sky.

Reach for me, be the moments I can't deny.

9:00am

Show Me

Do you love me she asks?
He silences her lips and looks into her eyes.
Do you love me she asks?
He holds her hands and strokes her thumbs.
Do you love me she asks?
He rubs his head with hers and kisses her nose.
And just as he begins to speak she softly whispers
shhhh...
Your actions are all ill ever need.
11:00pm

A Place Called Home

She feels like she needs more than a miracle to get her back to happy again.

Love is her outlet, it's the place where she finds the most comfort.

Love keeps her humble and sane and although it might seem crazy love is where she calls home.

1:00pm

Musical Love

16 Bars he spits to melt my heart.
Soulful up-tempo kisses that ride the beat.
Fantasizing about making love to his body.
Erotic music to numb his brain,
his concepts drive me insane.
4:52am

Sunrise to Sunset

Sunrises and I'm blinded by your love, that swee
embrace to hide me from my day.
As the clouds form they chase away the storm of
yesterday.
When the sunrises and sunsets all I am asking is
will you stay, and love me until the very next day
9:49pm

I Wanted More

He told me he wasn't afraid of anything and that he was left to be the man of the house, so he made sure he took on that role. At that moment, I believe I fell in love with him. I wanted to be fearlessly in love with him. I wanted to seek the knowledge he spoke of and explore the heights of his wildest dreams. At that moment I wanted more of him. I wanted less of what I had created in my fantasies and I wanted to see if he was truly meant for me.

3:49pm

Better Than
This

He enters my mind and clouds my thoughts. His intentions may very well be good, but he leaves me so confused. My mind plays tricks, and suddenly I'm lost within his grips. How did we end up back here on this merry go round?

Circles with no progress, I know for damn sure I should be sick of this but here I am not knowing when to call it a quits. That's my mistake. I should know I'm too grown for this. I'm way better than all of this shit.

Yet here I am lost in his Abyss.

9:10am

LOVING
YOU WAS A
FOOLISH
GAME THAT
I DECIDED
TO PLAY
LEASHA A. SMALL

New Feelings
of Love

New love can make you feel things one cannot explain. So filled with joy her happiness is evident. Overflowing, impossible to hide the feelings she feels. A glowing display, a reflection of love appears upon her face.

10:00am

Spinning Out of Control

You touch me and I lose control, you take on such a toll.
Passionate flames of burning love, you leave me all undone. A walking DJ of love.
Victim of sexual circumstance, you ignite the fire that makes me want to dance.
6:30am

Move On
They Say

I loved with my whole heart, and look where it left me, back at the very start. I loved you with all that am. I gave you all that I had. You took those years and you made a fool out of me, and still, I left you with all of your dignity. So tell me how could you do this to me after all these years?

How could you be so cruel?
How could you up and leave me in such misery?
Start over they say, accept, face, deal and walk away. Don't let the pain win.

Don't give in but how?

How does one erase the pain?

How does one move on from within?
My heart has only known you, so how do I go on living in this world without you?
8:19pm

Blast From The Past

A blast from the past, something that just wasn't built to last. There he is starring at me from across the room. I'm left in the moment when your feet are unable to move.

Hands cold, legs shaking, overall body feeling numb. He enters the room and I become so undone. I try to speak but nothing comes out, not even a peep, I had so much to say yet all the words had faded away. I try again but the only thing that comes out are the tears I held inside. The pain I faced is leaking out, all the years of reckless fights that turned into years of lonely nights. I knew I should have walked away letting him face the muted silence of words in which he'd long for me to say. The day I should have walked away but something was there that made me stay...

5:36am

Numb

Baby, I'm numb, numb to all your bullshit. Hoped that we could make it but I couldn't take it. Had me reppin while you were creeping. Tears down my face got me leaking, but that stream didn't bring healing. So I packed my shit and bounced quick, changed my number and said I was done with this. Showed up and said you weren't having it, too bad I was over this. Tired of looking like your fool I'm too grown for it.

12:19am

Holding On

You never make time for me but as soon as you're lonely that's when you know me.

I could never buy a moment of your time but now you're on the other end of the line.

Is this time different or can I expect a few weeks of playing where is Waldo?
Another game of hide and seek.
I truthfully don't have the time to play the games you're on.

That sh*t got old ten months ago, yet I still keep holding on.
7:17am

PAIN IS INEVITABLE SUFFERING IS OPTIONAL

M. KATHLEEN CASEY

Is It Me?

I'm slowly giving up, but something keeps pulling
me back.

Forcing myself to detach.

Breaking free from a bond that is no longer for me.
Tears I have cried, feelings I can't seem to deny.
All I ask is why?
Ruining my life.
Wasting my time.
Lies upon lies.
Why did you choose me?
Is it written on my forehead
Use me.
Abuse me.
Confuse me.
Am I the one to blame?
Should I hold my head in shame or is this part of
your game?
1:16pm

Place Of Peace

One glass of wine as I try to unwind. A long bubbl
bath as I lose track of time. An empty cold bed is
where I lay my head, and just to think I have to ge
up and do it all again. The stress of life is hard
enough, but to face this world without you by my
side is an even longer ride. Alone and there is no
place left for me to hide. No form of relief to ease
this tension building deep form inside, no partner
to provide that sense of peace that special place I
seek.

8:26pm

A Girl Like Me

Could you love a girl like me, one who is as fierce
and bold as me?
Could you love a girl like me, full of truth and
honesty?
Could you love a girl like me, one who is hard on
herself but never gives up hope?
Could you love a girl like me, who sees the world
like an open canvass to explore and roam free?
Could you love a girl like me, who has been
through the worst?
A girl like me who understands in order to find
love she has to be open to change.

3:17am

Heartbeat

I had so much going wrong but he loved me and kept holding on. You see he never gave up, he definitely wasn't one to call it a quits. I had so much pain but he took my hand and stood through the rain. I had cried so many tears and still, he wiped them clear. I had a broken heart so he gave me his hand and placed it on his heart and told me it was mine from the very start. He loved me back to life.

3:28pm

Believing On Empty

I was giving you someone to use, someone to
take advantage of, someone to abuse.
I was putting you first and in the midst
forgetting my worth.
I made it easy, all this giving never receiving.
In the end, I was empty, so when you left full of
course I was grieving.
I was the only one believing.
A one-sided love no you just me, only I was the
one who couldn't see, that you were wrong for
me.
10:53am

LOVE
YOURSELF
ENOUGH TO
WALK AWAY
FROM
ANYTHING
TOXICYOU
ARE YOUR
FIRST
PRIORITY
LEASHA A. SMALL

Try My Luck

The unlucky one.
The one who just can't seem to get it right, for love just never came on time. Love never seemed to come with the right guy, poor unlucky me right?
All the pain and hurt faced served as scars that wouldn't go away.
Still the unlucky one right?
Her past haunts and sometimes revisits burning visions of a horrible guy.
The unlucky one.
Just prayed for luck to be on her side, for her to meet the right guy. The one who would make it clear why it hadn't worked out with all those other guys.
The unlucky one, could this be a sign?
The unlucky one, could luck be on her side tonight?
8:08pm

Patiently Foolish

She waited patiently for things to change.
The thing was he never planned to evolve.

He was so stuck in his ways.
She hoped for better but didn't see those days
She lost herself within his false pretenses.
She did this to herself, why couldn't she see this.
Patiently waiting for a miracle, drowning in her
sorrows.
1:45am

I Quit

He never gave up on me but you see I did. I walked
away, more like I ran away, found a place to hide.
I never wanted him to see my broken pieces.
Shattered, you see I tried to piece myself together
but I was a hot ass mess. He loved me so much,
more than I could love myself. I was unable to give
him what he needed, an intern I became defeated.
A quitter, yes that's me walked away so unhappy
and it was all because of me.
9:12pm

TO LOVE OTHERS YOU MUST FIRST LOVE YOURSELF

LEO BUSCAGLIA

The Mistress

I shouldn't feel the way I do, but somehow all I keep thinking of is you. I obsess, I think, I cram my brain but what good does that do for me but drive me insane. I think about what the future holds but there is no story to be told, see that's where I unfold.
I lose myself, knowing I have absolutely no control, for our situation is beyond our reigns. So now what? Do I sit, wait and call upon faith. Do I beg and plead and hope that you choose me. I'm here hoping that things turn around. See, I never asked for this, I didn't plan on that kiss.
Somehow I'm the one stuck in all this mess when just one moment turned into all of this. What role do you play?
See I have never been the mistress, I never planned for this that night that ended with an ever-lasting kiss.
10:33pm

You Thought Wrong

I never needed you I was always stronger on my own, than beneath you.
You thought I would crumble when you took your love away, breaking under the pressure not able to remain okay. That was simply your mistake for I was destined to remain this way. No shade, I'm just simply stating, no man can break the mold that God has created. A prayer with some faith and he makes everything okay.

2:29am

TRUST YOUR
INSTINCTS
YOUR
INTUITION
DOESN'T LIE

LEASHA A. SMALL

Connected

Wavelengths of mind-blowing sexual tensions, our lines are now connected.

Miles away but still our time an attention is heavily invested.

He speaks sexual rhymes on the end of the line.

Giving me butterflies between my thighs, only he has the power to drive me wild.

He stands at attention as I speak of my unmentionable dripping confessions.

The ability to satisfy by a connection, a feeling we crave even miles apart we can ease this tension.

2:07am

I PrayedFor Love

So I prayed, you know for a love to find me and take my breath away. A love that lasts and is here to stay, a man that isn't perfect but owns his faults and works hard at them. A man who is open to love and isn't scared to put his pride aside in order to bring some form of order. A man who knows the value of his woman and the role he plays putting a smile on her face. A man who craves her touch, her smell, her love and would do anything just to be next to her. So when I tell you I prayed, know that I prayed for love and that love came to me as you!!

5:15am

Remember Us

The dreams we made, the house we paid for, the children we created and the goals we slaved for. Now look, what was all this for? If it was so easy for you to turn your back and close the door. Was she worth it, is this what your family deserves?
All this nonsense for your children to have to deal with. Did you know your son has nightmares and your daughter screams out for you? Forget about my tears that leave me awake at night, wondering how you could do this to me and our children and feel all right. It's me who has to comfort our children, hush them and tell them everything is going to be alright. Unsure of my damn self, what's to come of this mess, what am I to say?
Trying to be strong for our family, picking up the pieces you shattered. So when you kiss her remember the children you left behind. When you kiss her I hope my face haunts you. When you kiss her I hope you realize that all this is because of you.
Remember us when you're trying to recreate everything we've been through, everything we built. I hope karma bites you when you sit and think of us and all the neglect you put us through.
12:11am

Difficult To Love

He said I was difficult to love. He said I never acted like I needed anyone. He said I pushed him away and made him feel unloved. I never felt like I treated him this way and he never mentioned things weren't okay.

Was I so oblivious that I couldn't give that unconditional love, or so independent that I acted like I never wanted those hugs? Did I do this to myself? Pushing people away instead of asking for help. Show me how to love without reserve, show me how to trust and not constantly get on your nerves. Twenty-one questions of whose that girl when all you have ever shown me was that I was your one and only girl. So messed up from the past, I couldn't see your love was built to last. I have become a slave of my past.

1:18pm

Heartless Hustle

All she wanted was your time and attention. Too busy chasing the street life to notice you always came up missing. Is this the life you want to live? Full of the street riches but empty from within. She recognized your hustle even trusted your struggle, but it was you who couldn't be the pieces to her puzzle. You were lost from the very start. Counting money on the block didn't realize you were gambling with your very last shot.

5:25pm

What's Inside of You?

Speak to my inner Queen, take the time to inspire
me.

Dig deeper find what's below the surface, show me
you're here for a purpose.

Let the King in you reign true, be the best bold part
of you.

Open up and let me get to know you, the real deal
is what I'm trying to show you.

2:49pm

Black & Blue

She was tired of the pain, tired of pretending everything would be okay. Making excuses for how he would treat her but behind closed doors, all he use to do was beat her. This isn't love, love isn't made to make you feel this way. Full of pain she took to her grave, the day his fist connected to her dying day.

12:00am

SELF LOVE
SELF WORTH
SELF RESPECT
IT ALL STARTS WITH
YOU. DON'T LET
ANYONE ALLOW
YOU TO
COMPROMISE
THIS
LEASHA A. SMALL

CHECKMATE

He wants to be her **KING**
Although he acts like a **JOKER**
She whispers boy this is **CHESS**
Stop trying to play **POKER**
I'm the **QUEEN** just let me show ya.
Read the plays and lets get this
CHECKMATE.
4:30am

I Don't
F*ck With
You

Once you make me feel like I'm a bother to you, you can bet your bottom dollar ill fall back from you. See don't come back talking about "hey boo" because ill no longer have time for you. It's not about having a one up on you, it's more like I no longer got time to mess with you. Funny how things change just don't forget to stay in your lane... "Cause IDFWU" (Big Sean voice) 6:20pm

Alerts

Finally pressed send awaiting a response to end the
misery I feel on the receiving end.
Does he hate me?
Will he ignore me?
Is it too late to complete our story?
Memories flash through my mind as I press rewind,
our love was so divine.
My phone alerts, it's him.
Will this end in a negative or positive?
Story Time.
3:00pm

Reunited

The elevator opens he walks out, heart beating I'm speechless. With every step, my words are misplaced and all that's formed is the smile upon my face. From that day onward nothing was ever the same. That trip changed my last name.

12:19am

Rough Around
The Edges

He isn't one that's suggested. A little bit wreck les,
his flare is contested. Wild, this boy is forever on
the run. He needs to settle down, be a man and
wear a crown.
Focused on the social hype, instead of getting it
right. Always up to date with the newest drug.
When will this boy learn he can't be doing this
every night?
9:17pm

To Be Sure

I want to know my hearts sure, to be assured that
it's in good hands.
I want to be able to let down my guard and love
freely.
To know that the love given is solemnly all for me.
That I can trust not only your actions but what you
say to me.
I want to know that your love is a fighter and
despite any conflicts, you will be my rider.
To be able to count on our foundation, so that we
can continue building our bond.
A love like ours could be worth holding on.
A love like ours could be so strong.

1:09pm

Toxic Wasteman

Loving you is toxic, poison running deep within my veins.
Loving you is addictive, something I just can't shake.
Poisonous, toxic earthquake is the type of love we make.
11:32pm

Acting Alone

You made these decisions but where was I. You
formed these opinions and asked no questions.
You chose to struggle as if you were on your own.
Don't let your pride leave you single in our home.
We are suppose to work together, a unit, a team
just you and me.
7:02am

Don't Fail Me

He isn't ready to love me.
He isn't ready to be the man I need him to be.
All this time, this wasted time tryna get it right with
a man who isn't even meant to be by my side.
To listen to the heart that has failed me time and
time again.
To start over or to give it a try are the dilemmas
faced inside.
7:05am

Loves Disaster

I believed your promise because of the way my face would lit up when I heard your voice, or how the butterflies danced amongst my stomach each time you'd get close but silence themselves when we kissed. The way our memories seemed to bond us like glue. Intern, I'd make excuses for all your failed attempts, I seemed to be the fool. I mean I could go ahead and blame you for the way I'm feeling but ruthfully I blame myself. I now realize I owe myself an apology for not acknowledging my own worth. Accepting the little you threw at me to keep me holding on, playing puppet master as I moved my limbs to your song. I am the real fool for this love disaster, no more musical chairs. This isn't the kind of love I'm after.

2:03am

Locked Communication

If communication is key why wouldn't you choose to
unlock and set yourself free?
A slave to these chains, is your brain okay?
Break free, use the tools given and figure it out.
Don't bottle your feelings in, it's time to let them all
out.
Communication is the key why can't you see.
1:07pm

Him

My soul is searching, mind racing, heart beating,
feet pacing and all I can think about is you.
Tall, perfect smell, great build, dreamy eyes, heaven
sent, your everything and more.
A dream come true, could that be you.
You look into my eyes and my heart beat works
overtime.
A rhythm of love suddenly magnified.
12:53am

Love Under Construction

Through all the ups and downs of my heart, I believed in you and me.
Through all the pain and tears I still dreampt of a life full of happiness. It took time to grow to the place we're at now but when a love has a foundation nothing or no one can tamper with the structure.
So I am grateful for the construction.
I am grateful for the patience.
I am grateful for the love you give to me.
1:22pm

Broken Promises

I thought we made plans, I saw our future slip through the cracks.
Each word and memory left to vanish without a trace.
I believed you, I believed in us.
I saw our journey unfolding, only it wasn't the way we once pictured.
Things are completely different.
Just a place, no longer a home, no more you and I.
4:29pm

"TOLD YOU SO"

Sincerely,

Your Intuition

Unlovable

A repeat of unsettling déjà vu,
thought I was rid of it clearly, I hadn't learned from
the past.
Thinking that just maybe a change was going to
come.
Yet here I am with another rerun, just a reminder
of the past.
Just the same wreck less butterfly feelings ruining my
mind.
1:10pm

Bad Reception

When you are with me everything feels complete.
So why is it so difficult when mileage separates us
Why is it a constant struggle when we're apart?
One minute we're connected,
the next minute disconnected.
Bad reception?
No signal?
Are you even interested?
Questioning all the moments we shared.
Didn't you feel the chemistry or was it just me?
Can you hear me?
When I call you
Can you see it's me?
When I text you
Are you ignoring me?
4:11am

Work-o-holic

Yes, I work hard.
No, I don't have to choose.
If we're meant to be we will be.
Compromise I can do.
Asking me for more than you can give.
Sounds like an unfair motive.
1:11am

Despite It All

I loved him despite it all.
Took the good and the bad an loved him through it
all.
The ups the downs, nothing was ever promised to
be perfect but yet my heart knew he deserved it.
I gave him consistency, he gave me raw truths.
Somehow we found this unbreakable bond, a love
tied strong just us two.
1:08am

At Night

He enters my dreams and the walls close in.
My chest feels tight, the pressure building
my speech growing faint.
My soul screaming help, it's just this feeling that comes
over me.
This feeling I feel at night.
This feeling I just can't shake.
1:46am

Sometimes Home Is A Person

He's the one my heartbeats for, the one who makes me feel at home. The one who knows my soul and loves me whole. He's the one I was made for, my heart aligns for. I am the rib, God created perfectly for him. I know it's our time, this time is right.

He's the one I have waited for, the reason nothing else made sense. The reason my heart couldn't love from a distance, he's the reason others have failed, why love could never prevail. He's the one my heart desires, the one I require.

He's my Mr. Right the man that ignites my fire.

6:00am

The Calm To
My Chaos

He brought a calm sense to my chaos and inspite of it all he stuck through it. He held my hand not once giving up. I was never easy to handle, and I mean come on neither was he, but he loved me harder when I needed it and guided me closer when he felt the drift.

He took his time with our love, he was more than patient and in no time he became my other half. The one I couldn't live without, and he made sure I never had to. He was my forever without a doubt.

6:51pm

Hopeless
Romantic

Am I cursed?
This up and down rollercoaster.
Love & war it's become a battle.
Consistent ups and downs.
The good, the bad, the ugly and still I'm willing to
continue trying this love thing.
I know my time is coming.
I know my journey has just begun.
I know the one is out there for me
and I will continue to believe.
11:11pm

YOU ARE
MY FIRST
THOUGHT
AND MY
FAVORITE
PERSON
LEASHA A. SMALL

Positive Affirmations To Write Down For Yourself Regarding Relationships

I accept love & I deserve it

I will move forward with my life

I forgive those who have hurt me in the past

The love I extend returns to me in abundance

Love surrounds me

I love myself first

I am so grateful for the love that i have

My time is coming & love is on its way

I will respect my partner

I listen with an open heart and a clear mind

This year I choose myself

I will not be discouraged by love but embrace it

I will be more patient with myself on my journey

I embrace love

My relationships are filled with happiness

Everyday I miss my ex less

I deserve to be happy

Write Some of Your Own Positive Affirmations Regarding Relationships

A Letter To The Hopeless Romantic

Hey you... Yes you!!
The one reading and nodding, the one having flashbacks to memories similar to the ones that fill the pages. Situations good or bad are lessons to be learned. As long as we learn from these lessons we can grow from them.
Dear Hopeless Romantic your time is not up, it's not too late the right one is on his/her way.

Remember always that...
You are BLESSED
You are IMPORTANT
You are WORTHY
You are Loved

Leasha Angel Small
Ms. Diva416

This novel has been in the works since 2015.
I have always loved to write and I was thrilled to finally finish my first baby of many more to come. So thank you for taking this journey with me, and I hope you continue.
Stay tuned

Visit me at
@leashasmall
LeashaAngelSmall.wixsite.com